Don't Be a Chicken…
Ring the Bell

A Practical Handbook and Useful Guide for Selling Your Company

Douglas R. Palmer, CPA

DEDICATION

This book is dedicated to every successful entrepreneur who has trusted his or her legs to start and grow a business and now has decided to begin another chapter in life.

CONTENTS

Acknowledgments

Preface   Pg #1

Introduction   Pg #2

Deciding to Sell   Pg #6

Options for Selling   Pg #13

Sell!   Pg #16

Due Diligence   Pg #21

Financial Plan   Pg #29

Term Sheet   Pg #32

Definitive Agreement   Pg #40

Final Stages   Pg #46

Conclusion   Pg #51

ACKNOWLEDGMENTS

I am deeply thankful to the team of people who helped bring this book together. First, I would like to thank Lori Wark, who helped me with organizing, rewording, streamlining, and completing this project. Next, I am grateful to Tim Johnson, who served as a resource for this book. Finally, I would like to thank the folks in a number of different companies and service providers who have worked tirelessly to sell their companies and gave me the ideas for the material presented in this book.

PREFACE

If you've read *Don't Be a Chicken...Trust Your Legs*, you
know that a life-threatening event in my forties forced me
to reflect on what I really wanted to do with the rest of my
life. Knowing what could have been, I started putting into
action my dream of advising entrepreneurial companies.

Making my dream a reality wasn't always easy. I came up
against some pretty hefty bumps in the road, but I've never
looked back. In 2002 I started a financial consulting
practice. (We've been in business for over a decade!)

With this book, I'm paying my good fortune forward. I've
written this handbook for those of you who are thinking
about planning an exit strategy for your company but don't
know where to begin.

At the beginning of the handbook, I've listed key points,
which are discussed in the following chapter. At the end of
each chapter, I've listed questions to help you understand
how the information you've just read should be applied to
your particular business. Take time to consider your
answers. You may even want to write down your thoughts
and ideas. A written record of your learning process is a
great roadmap for creating a process to sell your business.

INTRODUCTION: THE WRONG WAY TO SELL A COMPANY

I firmly believe that any man's finest hour, the greatest fulfillment of all that he holds dear, is that moment when he has worked his heart out in a good cause and lies exhausted on the field of battle—victorious.
—Vince Lombardi

THREE KEYS
1. Clearly identify the reasons for selling your company. Begin with the end in mind. What does the exit look like, and how will you achieve this goal?
2. Be sure that only the right people represent your organization during integration meetings.
3. Stick to a rigid timetable.

It was the year 2000, and I had just started working for a high-tech firm as finance director. The company was booming, and my time there was the ride of a lifetime.

The company had three founders—Steve, George, and Adam—each with unique personalities. Intense Steve was the most charismatic but often the most disruptive. Like Steve Jobs of Apple, George was highly intelligent, but he was more levelheaded. He was your typical computer geek at a time when computer geeks were the coolest people in town. Adam was your professor type and was highly respected.

In 2000, I left PricewaterhouseCoopers, where I had seen companies and individuals making lots of money from the stock market. Millionaires were being made overnight as companies went public. Witnessing such wealth being made, I was inspired to join a start-up technology company. I wanted stock options, and I wanted to be there when the company went public. That's when I joined Steve, George, and Adam in their high-tech start-up.

I had made it. I had arrived. The company was going to grow, and I was on the road to becoming wealthy beyond my wildest dreams. As with all roads, however, a few bumps appeared, turning my dreams into a nightmare. Soon after I started my "dream job," the stock market collapsed and venture capitalists began pulling out of start-ups. The company's revenue declined, and it became apparent that our company was not going public, so a strategist was hired to investigate alternative solutions.

We hired Jim. Jim had rolled up a number of technology companies in the past and was aware of all kinds of strategic directions the company could pursue. Jim ultimately recommended to the founders that they look into selling the company as a way to take some risk off the table and create an exit strategy. The highly skilled employees would remain with the newly created organization. Everyone was comfortable with the decision, so Jim prepared the company to be sold. After many months and much hard work trying to find possible buyers, Jim did find a company that seemed perfect—a biotechnology firm that was looking for a solid development team to build its next generation of biotechnology products. Our team was excited to get into the biotechnology space and help change the world, but they also wanted to make a lot of money from the sale.

The negotiations started off well. Both sides were very interested, had similar goals, and wanted to work together—or so everyone thought.

But once at the table, it immediately became apparent that those negotiating from our company and those from the buyer's team were not clicking. Personalities clashed big-time.

Working to develop the term sheet, a major step in selling a company, which will be discussed later in this book, got bogged down. Time dragged on, and eventually the biotech firm walked away from the table.

Hindsight has crystallized for me what went wrong. We should have looked for multiple bids, which would have created a sense of urgency for the buyer to close the deal. When the teams weren't getting along, we should have replaced individuals to create a more congenial atmosphere. Also, allowing deadlines to slip gave the buyer time to walk away. Had I known more about the ins and outs of selling a company, I might be writing a happier ending to this story. That's why I'm writing this book.

I learned the hard way. Perhaps I can make it easier for those of you thinking about selling your company. Just knowing a few simple principles, understanding what steps to take, and being aware of the complex process you are about to face may make all the difference. My goal in writing this book is to help your story have a better ending.

STEP 1: DECIDING TO SELL

All the world's a stage, And all the men and women merely players. They have their exits and their entrances, And one man in his time plays many parts...
—William Shakespeare

FOUR KEYS

1. Be sure that selling the company is the right thing to do. Complete a presale questionnaire.

2. Perform a business sales analysis and a "sell now or later" analysis.

3. Perform a personal finance analysis.

4. Review your values and future life expectations before venturing to sell. Is now the right time from a personal perspective?

After more than forty years as a high school English

teacher, my mother decided to retire. In her retirement speech, she quoted a line from William Shakespeare's *As You Like It*, which describes life as a stage with multiple entrances and exits. My mother reflected that while she was exiting the teaching profession, she was now entering a new stage of her life with new possibilities, one of which was being a grandmother. Business, like life, is full of chapters. One chapter of your life is going to be owning your current business. One key to owning this business is knowing when the chapter should come to an appropriate ending.

Just like when you began your business and you took a good look at why you wanted to start your own company, what values you wanted to bring to the workplace, and whether your chosen field would be fulfilling to you, taking a deep look at your motivations for selling is just as critical. The following are steps you should take before making the big decision:

Step One: Self-Analysis

The first step is to ask yourself, "Do I even want to sell?" Don't assume selling is right for you just because it seems to be the latest flavor of the month. If you love your work and your business gives you joy in holding the reins, as your "baby" becomes a mature company, selling may not be in the cards for you. Maybe you are tired of the grind, the work is no longer inspiring, and you're looking to move on to other interests and passions. Then the moment to sell might have arrived. Perhaps, you want to remain connected to the company in some capacity but without the headaches that come with managing a business. Crafting a deal that works for you is not out of the question. In fact, many buyers are looking for a ready-made, experienced team as part of the deal.

Step Two: Business Analysis

Even when the decision to sell is made, the timing may not be ideal. If your company is in the middle of a revenue downturn because of the economy or structural issues within the business, it may not be the best time to look for potential buyers. If, however, your company is experiencing growth month after month, not selling now could be a missed opportunity.

How your business is set up also influences your decision. If you have partners, getting their input on such a major shift in the future of the company is imperative.

Step Three: Personal Finances Analysis

Don't forget to evaluate your personal financial situation. Will you be set for life after the sale, or do you need to find other sources of income? In addition, consider the tax hit. If you sell your company now, will you be paying long-term capital gains or is the deal going to result in a higher tax rate? Long-term capital gains are assessed on assets that have been held for more than a year. The ordinary income tax rate is based on your income tax bracket (which would normally be much higher than the capital gains rate).

Step Four: Selling Now or Later Analysis

How much money you gain from the sale also depends on a projection of your potential income. If you sell your business now and you would have had a growth spurt, the cash you would have made would grow exponentially and yield more money than selling your business. If projection forecasts for the coming year are that revenue will remain flat, you could see a bigger windfall with a sale. Selling when the time is right is important.

Stage Five: Your Future Analysis

The thought of selling your company for a big payday may sound enticing; however, money should not be the sole factor when negotiating to sell your business.

Take a hard look at your motivations and how you want to control and shape your future. What's next for you? Are you looking forward to starting a new company? Is retirement the next chapter? Are you dreaming of spending your days golfing or learning something new, or is your goal to spend more time with your family? Is mentoring or giving time to future entrepreneurs a new ambition? Are you the type of person who will get bored with too much time on your hands?

Step Six: Intangible Analysis

In addition, remember the intangibles: your values, your passions, and your dreams. Refer to *Don't Be a Chicken—Reach for the Stars: A Practical Handbook to Growing Your Company…and Life at the Same Time* for help in organizing your core values into a balance wheel. A balance wheel is a visual representation of your core values and can help you understand where the selling of your company fits into your life.

Along with creating a balance wheel, the tried and true listing of pros and cons is a great way to put down your thoughts so you can see the positives and negatives of selling.

Step Seven: Pros and Cons List

"My Way is, to divide half a Sheet of Paper by a Line into two Columns, writing over the one Pro, and over the other Con. Then during three or four Days Consideration I put down under the different Heads short Hints of the different Motives that at different Times occur to me for or against the Measure. When I have thus got them all together in one View, I endeavour to estimate their respective Weights; and where I find two, one on each side, that seem equal, I strike them both out: If I find a Reason pro equal to some two Reasons con, I strike out the three…thus proceeding I find at length where the Balance lies; and if after a Day or two of farther Consideration nothing new that is of Importance occurs on either side, I come to the Determination accordingly."

—Letter to John Priestly from Benjamin Franklin, 1772

Although Ben Franklin's take on a pros and cons list may seem like an algebraic equation, taking the time to create and analyze the pros and cons of selling a business or making any other life choice as methodically as Franklin will likely uncover the best answer. Two ideas to notice in Franklin's method is how carefully he weighs each pro and con and balances them against each other, crossing off those of equal weight. In this way, he narrows the field of competing ideas. He also allows time. Franklin's list evolves over days and weeks and is not an exercise to be undertaken during a quick coffee break.

Another option is to create a decision tree instead of a two-column list. A decision tree is a treelike graph with "branches" representing various decisions and their possible outcomes. Software programs are now available to help with creating a decision tree.

Handbook Questions:

- Have you performed a self-analysis before you sell your company?
- Have you carefully considered the market for selling your business? Is the timing right? Should you wait for a better time?
- Have you written a pros and cons list?

STEP 2: OPTIONS FOR SELLING

Your time is limited, so don't waste it living someone else's life…And, most important, have the courage to follow your heart and intuition.
—Steve Jobs

THREE KEYS
1. Decide in advance if you want to keep working as an employee for your company.
2. Consider all available options for your exit before starting the process.
3. Proceed with the exit only after thinking through and agreeing on all options.

When negotiating with a buyer, look beyond the dollars and cents. The deal for structuring a sale can take many forms. Below are a few formats a deal can take.

Become an employee. Will a sale hinge on your continuing to work for the company as an employee for a number of years with the stipulation that you bring in a certain percentage of the business each year? For some people this may be a good deal. Some of the happiest people I know who have sold their company continue to be involved in some capacity. While the responsibility and stress of being the head honcho is now over, they still have their toe in the pool in guiding the business, and they take home a paycheck. If your goal is to remain actively involved in the company, the duration of your employment term, your title in the new company, and how many people you will manage are all things to be carefully thought through.

Stay involved. If you like what you're doing and want to keep at it, you may want to consider selling only a piece of the company. One of my clients, a booming professional services business, decided to do just that. The partners in the firm enjoyed their work, but they wanted to take some risk off the table so they sold a piece of their company to a private equity group. With this strategy, they were able to monetize a portion of the business while continuing to grow the portion of the company that remained theirs to operate.

Cut the strings. If the above deals make you feel like you would be entering a dark tunnel of continuing burnout, a clean break should be your goal.

Begin again. Perhaps you're looking for that adrenaline rush of starting a new business. If your sights are on creating a company in the same industry as or a similar industry to the company you are selling, take a look at any non-compete clauses, which may limit your choice of industries within a certain time frame.

Handbook Questions:

- Have you carefully decided if you will become an employee?
- How long do you plan to stay employed with the new firm?
- Are you considering starting another company in the same industry?

STEP 3: SELL!

Art is making something out of nothing and selling it
—Frank Zappa

THREE KEYS
1. Hire an investment banker right away.
2. Make sure the investment banker knows your industry and is familiar with all the players.
3. Use a transactional lawyer (as opposed to a general business lawyer).

Yⁱ
ou've gone through all the pros and cons, identified your core values, have an idea of the best deal for you, and now you're ready to sell. What next?

Step One: DIY or Investment Banker

Your next decision is whether you should do it yourself or hire an investment banker. Going it alone with deals that can become very complex is not a good idea. Hire an investment banker who can shepherd you through the process and give you sound advice.

Step Two: Find an Investment Banker

The selection of an investment banker is extremely important. Bankers generally specialize in certain industries. If you choose a banker with the wrong industry experience, you may be put in contact with buyers who are not interested in companies in your particular industry. Talk to a number of bankers and find out their backgrounds—and whether they have closed multiple deals with companies in your industry space. Also, if your business is heavily involved in technology, make sure your banker understands that technology, at least to some extent.

Typically, bankers like to charge a monthly retainer and then receive a commission based on the sale. This is most likely the best fee structure with one caveat—make sure the monthly retainer is not exorbitant. A retainer that's on the low end will keep the banker motivated to getting the deal done. Try to negotiate the lowest monthly retainer you can.

The banker will also ask for exclusivity when representing your firm for a sale. This is fine; however, you need to be able to seek out another banker if the current one is found to be unsuitable. Aim for the least restrictive exclusivity clause as possible, and try to keep the contract period to no more than three to six months so you are not tied down to the wrong banker for too long.

The following are ways an investment banker will make your life easier:

Market Trends. A banker will take a look at the market trends. A market analysis of current trends will tell you if it's a good time to sell and if so, what type of deal will make your company more attractive to potential buyers. Most importantly, a market analysis will give you an idea of how much your company is potentially worth.

Process. The banker will set out a formal process and a timeline for each step—from receiving bids to closing the deal. Without a timeline, deals can drag on. If deadlines slip the more chance the deal will never get done. This is exactly the scenario describe in the introduction of this book.

Intention. The decision to hire an investment banker makes a statement to you as well as to potential buyers that you are serious about selling your company.

Competition. Creating a competitive situation will work in your favor. Bankers are business brokers who are constantly talking to a wide range of people interested in buying companies. This pool of potential buyers immediately creates a competitive atmosphere. With multiple bids you are more assured of getting the market value for your company.

Deadlines. A banker will establish a certain process, have deadlines, and make sure every party sticks to them. Deadlines are key to making sure that a deal gets completed.

Multiple Offers. The banker will put together an offering packet or a booklet to send to a number of prospective buyers to attract multiple suitors. Aside from generating multiple offers, a banker will also help evaluate each individual company and help you decide which offer best fits your goals.

In the case I related in the introduction, there was only one offer to work with at the time, which proved to be a disastrous situation. If there had been multiple offers, the outcome could have been different. A suitor has no sense of urgency when he is the only one bidding. This enables the negotiations to take an inordinate amount of time, which can be a death knell for a deal.

Advice. An investment banker will become your closest and most trusted adviser. During the weeks and months of finding and negotiating with buyers, you will need someone to talk to, get advice from, strategize with, and eventually close the deal. An investment broker can also introduce you to a good legal team to help with the legal aspects of a sale.

Step Three: Find a Transactional Lawyer

The selection of a good law firm is also extremely important. The law firm that you use to sell your company will most likely not be the same firm that represents you in your daily corporate matters. The lawyers for your deal should be solely traction oriented and should specialize in completing tractions in your industry.

Just like when evaluating investment bankers, you want to talk to a number of law firms and find out each firm's industry experience—and whether they have completed multiple transactions with companies in your space.

The sale of your company is most likely the largest asset you have—so make sure you take your time when selecting a law firm (and do not just go with your current firm because it is the easiest thing to do).

Handbook Questions:

- Have you thoroughly researched and engaged a banker who knows your industry?
- Has your banker closed deals in your industry?
- Have you evaluated law firms? Are your lawyers specialized in completing transactions in your industry?

STEP 4: DUE DILIGENCE

Diligence is the mother of good luck.
—Benjamin Franklin

FOUR KEYS

1.Be thoroughly prepared before due diligence. Take care of all potential diligence issues before you attempt to sell your company.

2.Make sure your company representatives are "people-oriented" and can get along with the other side.

3.Ensure that your company has no tax and/or regulatory issues before going through diligence.

4.Stay focused on running your company, and let the bankers handle the diligence process.

Due diligence is the process whereby a potential buyer will perform an in-depth investigation of a company and its assets before signing on the dotted line. Some important things to remember:

Lookin' good. Having been a CPA for two decades, I know the importance of having books and records that look good at first glance and can survive a deeper look. To present the best possible face to a potential buyer, make sure your financial records are in order. Messy books set the stage for buyers to question other parts of the business. Engage a CPA to make sure everything looks perfect. Any deliverables to be given to the potential buyer must be in pristine order. Check and recheck anything you plan to put before the person you are courting.

Questions and more questions. There's more to due diligence than just peering into financials. The potential buyer might inquire about your human resource practices as well as possible liabilities and legal issues that are outstanding. He may look at how you're paying your employees and what methods you are using to keep track of time.

Questions about the types of software you're using for all aspects of the business may also come up. Be prepared to answer a lot of questions. If there are any potential red flags, take care of these issues before you attempt to sell. Not doing so may lower the valuation of your company or, even worse, crater a deal.

Your employees. Make sure you are paying your employees a decent salary, especially during due diligence. You will be asking your employees to take on extra work gathering files, creating reports, and researching questions asked by potential buyers. Besides the extra work, selling a company can be stressful for those who work for the company. There may be insecurity about what will happen to their job once the company is sold, so consider setting up a sale bonus for your employees when a deal closes. You want your employees to be on your side during diligence so there is no temptation on the part of your staff to sabotage the deal.

Here is an example of typical due diligence questions (see a full diligence questionnaire example in appendix A):

I.   General

- Copies of internal financial management reports (i.e. weekly/monthly status reports).

II.   Financial Planning

- Fiscal year 200x/y budgets.
- Revenue projections for 200x/y.
- Current business plan.
- Cash flow forecasting for 200x/y.
- Current "pipeline" analysis.

III. Cash Management

- Current bank balance.
- Average bank balance per month.
- Monthly "burn" amount (in total and by department).
- List of banks and investments.
- Policies regarding investment of idle cash balances.

IV. Receivable Management

- Analysis of total receivables (broken down by customer, employees, officers, etc).
- Current aged accounts receivable listing.
- Current credit policies and trade terms for customers.
- Method used to establish allowance for doubtful accounts.
- Procedures for collection of outstanding accounts receivable.

V. Property & Equipment

- Detailed summary of P&E and accumulated depreciation (i.e. detailed FA register).
- Schedule of capitalized leased equipment.
- Listing of leased equipment accounted for as an operating lease.
- Record of obsolete equipment.

- Analysis of office space currently being leased and sublet.

VI.   Liabilities

- Schedule of current liabilities by category (i.e. trade, accrued, etc).
- Listing of major suppliers.
- Line of credit details.
- Detail for equipment loan facility.
- Schedule of deferred revenue.
- Listing of all material contractual commitments.

VII.   Taxes

- Company tax returns for the past three years.
- Federal/State reports or other correspondence within the last three years.
- Listing of any tax disputes in the past three years.
- Listing of states for which sales and use tax has been paid.

VIII.   Revenue

- Schedule of revenue by customer.
- Listing of major customers and any analysis of customer's financial condition.
- Ranking of sales personnel by revenue volume (i.e. top performers and how much volume).
- Analysis of commissions paid to sales personnel.

IX. Contracts

- Copies of all material contracts in force.
- Listing of all pending contracts.
- Copies of all governmental contracts (if any).

X. Market Data

- Breakdown of sales and market coverage geographically.
- Market share data (if available).
- Number and names of repeat clients.

XI. Operations

- Description of invoicing process (i.e. when invoicing performed, when sales personnel are compensated, etc).
- Current time keeping system information.
- How receivable collection is monitored.
- Current accounting software system information.

XII. Other

- Listing of current insurance coverage.
- Any pending or threatening litigation not yet disclosed.
- D&B information.

Getting Along. When going through due diligence and the term sheet process, you want to make sure that the people who are coming to the table can get along. In the introduction to this book, I told the story of a deal that flopped. One of the issues was that at a meeting of buyers and sellers it was obvious the two sides did not click. In hindsight it would've made more sense to reevaluate the company's selected negotiators to find people who were more like-minded to the buyer representatives. As I've said before, the process of selling a company can be long and arduous. Everyone coming to the table needs to get along. A banker can give you advice if a clash of personalities occurs.

Regulatory Risk. There may also be governmental factors or regulatory risk that comes into play while due diligence is in process. A banker can make you aware if the government has decided to start focusing on a specific industry or making changes to an industry that could negatively affect the valuation of your company or the deal itself. A banker will also keep you up to date on any regulations that could affect a deal.

External Forces. On the acquirer's side, other external forces may also come into play during due diligence. For example, if a publicly traded company is looking to purchase your company and something goes on at the company that sidetracks the deal though it's unrelated to you or the team, the negotiations could stall or end entirely. A banker will advise you if such a situation occurs.

Taxes. In my early days at Price Waterhouse I worked on a couple of due diligence assignments. The number one finding during the due diligence review was an adverse tax situation. So before you attempt to attract buyers, make sure your state and federal taxes are up-to-date and there are no outstanding tax liabilities. Have your CPA also look at all tax documents and correspondence so he or she can verify your tax compliance, including payroll taxes.

The key thing to remember during any due diligence is to stay focused on your company and let the bankers and CPAs run the due diligence process.

Handbook Questions:

- Have you gone through your books with your CPA before going through due diligence?
- Are there any known tax and/or regulatory issues that need to be addressed before going into due diligence?
- Have you evaluated your human resources processes? Have you inspected the employees files and are there any looming issues that need to be addressed before due diligence?
- Do you have the best company representatives working with the other side during the due diligence process?

STEP 5: FINANCIAL PLAN

If you want to reap financial blessings, you have to sow financially.
—Joel Osteen

THREE KEYS
1. Be realistic with your financial plan.
2. The financial plan should be accurate and very close to actual for the next six months.
3. Let your CPA or banker create and maintain your financial plan and projections.

While going through due diligence, the potential acquirer will typically ask for projections and a financial plan. Make sure you have detailed one- and five-year financial plans. In my book *Don't Be a Chicken...Trust Your Legs*, I discussed how to put together a five-year plan. Refer to that book for an in-depth discussion.

Some rules of thumb in creating your five-year financial plan are:

Get advice. Hire a CPA to work up the financial plans. They have the experience and will be more levelheaded in putting the figures together than you, since they don't have the same investment in the outcome as you do.

Be realistic. Don't lowball or ignore expenses just to look good. Revenue projections should be accurate and tied to specific metrics.

Be accurate. The five-year plan should show current numbers and future projections. The deal process and the sale process is long and can go on for months, so your projections have to be spot-on for at least the next six months. If a potential buyer during negotiations compares your actual numbers with what you have projected and there is a significant discrepancy, the buyer may scale back the offer or walk away from the deal.

Be proactive. Don't assume that because you glanced at

your books everything is in order. Have a banker take a deep dive into your books. A banker can easily spot pitfalls and advise you on additional information buyers typically want to see.

Be hands-off. Don't micromanage. Once you hire a banker and a CPA, let them do what they do best so you can get on with the process of closing a deal.

Be sure: It's also important to perform due diligence on any potential buyers. You want to be sure an interested party can realistically purchase your company before you go too far in the negotiations and waste time. Make sure any candidates are financially in a position to purchase and that their business practices are trustworthy.

Handbook Questions:

- Do you have a financial plan to present in due diligence that is realistic?
- Does your financial plan closely represent reality for the foreseeable future?
- Has an external person helped to create and maintain the financial plan/projections?

STEP 6: TERM SHEET

Every sale has five basic obstacles: no need, no money, no hurry, no desire, no trust.
—Zig Ziglar

THREE KEYS
1. Let your CPA handle the diligence requests for financial information.
2. Keep the lawyers "at bay" when negotiating a term sheet.
3. Continue to run your business and let the bankers and professionals run the diligence process.

At the same time due diligence is going on, a term sheet is also being created. A term sheet is a bullet-point document that lays out the preliminary terms of an agreement. A term sheet is a nonbinding document that serves to lay out the intentions of both parties. Once the parties are in agreement with the terms listed, a lawyer can draw up the final agreement. Some items that will be included in the term sheet are:

• How the purchase will be made (stock, cash, or a combination).
• Legal structure to be used for the sale.
• Approximate dates of due diligence.
• Which party is responsible for expenses.
• Specifics of how much the acquiring company will pay you for any time you become an employee with the new organization.
• Which employees will become part of the new company.

Negotiations over a term sheet can be a make-or-break situation. Some key points to remember are:

Keep it moving. It's important to keep the process going and not get too hung up on the small points that could stop a deal in its tracks. Don't give away the farm, but be open to compromise.

Keep the business going. Don't let your business suffer as you're going through negotiations. Let the bankers deal with the deal and answer buyer questions so you can stay focused on your company. Going down the tubes at this time would not be a good selling point.

Keep your CPA in the loop. Interested buyers are likely to ask for lots of documents—financial records, human resource records, employee withholding, and legal records. A buyer may also ask for an audit. Let your CPA handle these requests.

Keep lawyers at bay. Although lawyers are a necessary part of evaluating and advising on the term sheet, try to keep lawyers out of the discussions. Lawyers have a tendency to insert legalese that can muddy the waters and sour the deal. Don't get me wrong; lawyers are very important when selling your company, and you will need a good law firm to help with the final agreement. However when you're negotiating the initial points for the term sheet, lawyers can add some unneeded complexity to the discussions.

During negotiations it will seem very easy to pick up the phone and call your lawyer every step of the way. No matter how brief a call, it costs money. Talk to your lawyer about setting up a flat fee instead of an hourly rate for his or her services. This will help you budget better and not run up a tab without being aware of the dollars mounting until you get the bill.

Keep to deadlines. Time is of the essence, and setting deadlines will help you keep on track. A deal that should take two to three months to close can easily slip to six to nine months. When the process starts to drag on for that much time, the deal usually doesn't get done.

Keep your cash. Some interested buyers may suggest

they would like to use your cash to purchase your company. The usual deal is that the buyer will purchase with your money and give you a bonus to sweeten the deal. A proposal such as this is in effect using your money to purchase your company, a scenario to be avoided.

Keep it happy. It's important to remember when creating the term sheet, which will inform the final deal, that both sides must be happy with the outcome. Wanting to make as much money as possible is natural, but the reality of the situation is if the buyer is not happy at closing, things can happen after the deal that could negatively affect your employment with the new company if you have decided to stay.

Keep your values. While in the midst of putting a term sheet together, it's easy to forget why you started this process. Review you balance wheel and your pros and cons list. Keep in mind the values and beliefs you hold dear and don't get sidetracked. Keep focused on your values, and what you ultimately want to gain from this transaction.

When the deal closes, you want to walk away feeling you have been as honest and trustworthy as possible when answering the buyer's questions.

Don't bank in your head. Banking in your head is a phrase that describes when you start counting the dollars and dreaming of how the dough will be spent when the funds materialize. Banking in your head takes your focus away from the task at hand. Stay on track and close the deal.

It's a good idea not to tell spouses or significant others

about the possible deal or the potential pot of money. There's just too many valuables and factors that can cause a deal to go south to get hopes up prematurely, which could cause more distractions when you're trying to get the deal done.

Negotiate a break-up fee. Breaking up shouldn't be easy to do. It's important to negotiate in the term sheet a break-up fee, which is an agreed-upon payment if one of the parties decides to back out. The fee covers such expenses as lawyers, CPAs, resources used, and time spent.

Make a plan B. OK, you've gone through the due diligence piece, you are close to satisfying all the conditions, and are close to signing a definitive agreement. It looks like the deal is going to go through!

Be aware, however, that a large percentage of deals in the midst of due diligence and even during the final agreement phase will ultimately not close. That's when plan B comes into play. Develop a plan B at the same time you start working on your plan A. If your first plan ultimately does not work out, your second plan will be there for you.

A plan B may simply entail selling the company to the existing management for a price close to the initial deal price. A more involved plan B may be to keep the negotiations going with a second interested party concurrently with the first-party negotiations.

Remember your employees. Let's face it. The reason you have been so successful in your business is not only your drive, ambition, and managerial skills, it's also the people you've hired who became devoted employees and who also contributed to a successful enterprise. Some employees may have been with you during the struggling start-up days and are still contributing, making your company worthy of attracting buyers.

Make sure the deal stipulates such items as:

• Will salaries remain the same or increase?
• Will employees need to travel to a distant location or possibly move?
• What will happen regarding the retirement and health insurance benefits?
• Will there be stock options?
• Can employees work remotely?

Here is an example of term-sheet provisions from an example term sheet (source: The Musings of the Big Red Car):

Purchase price: The Purchase Price shall be $x00,000,000 together with the cash on hand plus the difference between net receivables and net payables at the time of the closing of the transaction.

Payment terms: The Purchase Price shall be paid in accordance with the following schedule.

-Cash down payment: $x00,000,000

-Promissory note   The delivery of a Promissory Note in the initial balance of the Purchase Price minus the Cash Down payment.

-Term of the Promissory Note: X years

-Interest rate: X% per annum

-Amortization period: X years

-Payment frequency: Monthly/Quarterly/Annually

-Payment: $X

-Collateral, guaranty: Describe the collateral or guaranty of the Promissory Note here.

Asset Sale and Purchase Agreement: The parties will enter into a binding Asset Sale and Purchase Agreement incorporating the terms of this Letter of Intent. Nothing in this Letter of Intent shall be binding except for the Confidentiality provision.

Due diligence materials: The Seller will deliver to the Buyer a complete package of due diligence materials as enumerated in the Asset Sale and Purchase Agreement within seven (7) days of the effective date of the agreement.

Due diligence period: 30 days from the receipt of the last due diligence materials

Closing date: 30 days after the conclusion of the due diligence period

Earnest money deposit: 5% of the Purchase Price

Employment agreements: As a condition to closing, the

Buyer will enter into Employment Agreements with critical personnel including, but not limited to, the CEO, COO, CFO of the Seller.

Contingency: This Letter of Intent is an offer to sell by the Seller and shall be accepted, if desired, by the Buyer. This Letter of Intent is intended only to outline the business terms of the Asset Sale and Purchase Agreement referred to in this document. Other than the Confidentiality provision and the exclusivity terms, nothing in this Letter of Intent is binding upon the parties.

Handbook Questions:

- Have you engaged a CPA firm that will prepare your financial documents and handle your diligence requests?
- Have you negotiated a flat fee arrangement with your law firm? Have you set the expectation with the law firm that your banker will negotiate the key terms on the term sheet?
- Have you developed a plan B if the current deal falls through?
- Have you done due diligence on the buyer?

STEP 7: DEFINITIVE AGREEMENT

Unless both sides win, no agreement can be permanent.
—Jimmy Carter

THREE KEYS
1.Work with your law firm to ensure appropriate representations and warranties.
2.Make sure that the covenants are not too restrictive.
3.Do your due diligence to ensure the buyer financing to pay for the deal is not too burdensome.

You are now in the final stages of your deal. You have passed the Due Diligence Phase and are now beginning to negotiate a Definitive Agreement. Unlike the term sheet, which is not binding, the definitive agreement is final.

A definitive agreement is usually a fifty-to-eighty-page document that spells out with specific legalize the items agreed upon in the term sheet. The lawyers on both sides usually spend a lot of time on this agreement.

Here are some things to look out for:

Representations, warranties & indemnification. Representations and warranties occur according to a set schedule during the process of due diligence. This is the time to air all dirty laundry and be up front about the good and the bad.

The seller is obligated to warrant that the company is in compliance with all governmental laws and regulations and that there is no pending litigation, taxes have been filed properly, and that you are, in fact, the owner of the company.

If the buyer ultimately discovers after purchase that any financial statements, reports, or descriptions about the company have been misrepresented and the buyer has a loss due to these misrepresentations, they have the right to get their money back for the purchase of your company.

Stock deals. If stock is involved in the selling of a company, the buyer assumes all liabilities both past, present, and future. If reps and warranties are untrue and the buyer has a loss, you could possibly pay a large fee.

Indemnification. The clause on indemnification will outline what the remedies are for the party that incurs a loss. These reps and warranties are put in a different bucket. What would you be on the hook for post-acquisition in the event of a breach, and how long are you on the hook?

Covenants. Similar to debt covenants when raising company debt, the seller may be required to stick to certain covenants before the deal closes. For example, the seller may not be allowed to spend over a certain amount of capital expenses, selling off assets or issuing large bonuses. This section is designed to make sure that the seller does not "clean out" the company assets right before it is acquired.

Financing. This is relevant if the buyer is purchasing your company with debt. The buyer may have to describe in detail its source of funds. It is important to understand the buyer's debt load post-deal and ensure that the purchasing company will be solvent after the deal (especially if an earn-out is involved as part of the purchase price).

Closing conditions. This part condenses what must happen for the deal to finally close. It is a summary of most of the earlier sections.

Transactional lawyer. When going through this

process, you need to hire a transactional lawyer that is experienced. You wouldn't go to a foot doctor if you had a brain injury. Hiring the right transactional lawyer is one of the most important decisions you will make when you are looking to sell your company.

Here is the table of contents for a sample seventy-four-page definitive agreement:

Section 1. The Offer
  The Offer
  Company Actions
  Directors
Section 2. Merger Transaction
  Merger of Purchaser into the Company
  Effect of the Merger
  Closing; Effective Time
  Merger Without Meeting of Stockholders
  Certificate of Incorporation and Bylaws;
        Directors and Officers
  Conversion of Shares
  Surrender of Certificates; Stock Transfer Books
  Appraisal Rights
  Further Action
Section 3. Representations and Warranties of the Company
  Due Organization; Subsidiaries, Etc.
  Certificate of Incorporation and Bylaws; Minutes
  Capitalization, Etc.
  SEC Filings; Financial Statements
  Absence of Changes
  Title to Assets
  Real Property; Equipment
  Intellectual Property
  Contracts
  Liabilities
  Compliance with Legal Requirements
  Regulatory Matters
  Product Registration Files
  Certain Business Practices
  Communications
  Tax Matters

Employee Matters; Benefit Plans
Environmental Matters
Insurance
Transactions with Affiliates
Legal Proceedings; Orders
Authority; Binding Nature of Agreement
Section 203 of the DGCL, Etc. Not Applicable
Vote Required
Non-Contravention; Consents
Fairness Opinion
Financial Advisor
Conflict Minerals
Disclosure
Section 4. Representations and Warranties
Due Organization
Purchaser
Authority; Binding Nature of Agreement
Non-Contravention; Consents
Disclosure
Absence of Litigation
Funds
Ownership of Company Common Stock
Section 5. Certain Covenants of the Company
Access and Investigation
Notification of Certain Events
Operation of the Company's Business
No Solicitation
Third Party Notices
Section 6. Additional Covenants of the Parties
Filings and Approvals
Company Options, Company RSUs,
     Company PSUs, Company Stock Awards, ESPP Purchase Rights
Employee Benefits
Compensation Arrangements
Indemnification of Officers and Directors
Security holder Litigation
Third Party Consents
Treatment of Convertible Senior Notes
Disclosure
Resignation of Directors
Takeover Laws; Advice of Changes
Section 16 Matters
Stock Exchange Delisting; Deregistration

Financing
Section 7. Conditions Precedent to The Merger
No Restraints
Consummation of Offer
Section 8. Termination
Termination
Effect of Termination
Expenses; Termination Fee
Section 9. Miscellaneous Provisions
Amendment
Waiver
No Survival of Representations and Warranties
Entire Agreement; Counterparts
Applicable Legal Requirements; Jurisdiction;
     Specific Performance; Remedies
Assignability
Third Party Beneficiaries
No Recourse to Financing Sources
Notices
Cooperation
Severability
Obligation of Parent
Construction
Exhibit A
Certain Definitions
Annex I
Conditions of the Offer

Handbook Questions:

- Have you worked with a lawyer to appropriately establish representations and warranties?
- Have you done due diligence on the buyer's financing of the deal?
- Have you explored all types of purchase arrangements to ensure the best tax position?
- Do you have the best transactional lawyer to help through the deal process?

STEP 8: FINAL STAGES

Progress comes from the intelligent use of experience.
—Elbert Hubbard

FOUR KEYS

1. Evaluate your tax situation again before the deal closes.

2. Meet with or hire a financial planner before the deal closes.

3. Create a financial plan for the funds to be received.

4. Evaluate and explore the post-deal environment before the deal closes.

Y ou are now in the final stages of selling your company. What now?

Tax exposure. Consider your tax exposure well in advance of the deal closure.

Even though you may have filed your company tax returns and are compliant with federal and state tax regulations, the sale of your company may result in necessary tax filings in multiple states and include amounts not previously estimated and duly paid. Usually, the seller has paid the necessary amount in his own state but incorrect amounts in other states. When going through due diligence, this may be discovered, which can make negotiations at the end complicated or in need of a larger amount placed in escrow (which is not good for the seller).

Adverse tax situations can be even worse after the deal closes. Usually, the definitive agreement contains a clause that states that the seller represents that it is not aware of any adverse tax situations. If it becomes clear that there is a significant amount of tax owed at the time of the sale, the seller is usually obligated to pay the tax.

After the sale, the seller is no longer in control of the company and usually cannot take over control of the process of working with state regulators to rectify the situation. As such, the seller then must rely on the new owner to represent the company during the audit. This puts the seller in a big disadvantage. In addition, if the seller is obligated to pay the tax and the money is in escrow, the new owner has no real incentive to dispute the tax situation. As such, he may not give this the same level of attention that the seller would. This may not be in the seller's best interest and can possibly lead to a legal dispute between the seller and the buyer.

Make a financial plan. The sale of your business may result in the largest lump sum of money that you have ever had. Make sure you hire a financial planner to help you come up with a plan for the proceeds of the deal before the close of the deal. It is extremely important that you give some thought to how the funds will be allocated and invested before even receiving any proceeds.

I have seen situations in which a business owner sold his company and left the entire amount in cash in a money market account for more than a year (in which the stock market rose more than 20 percent). I have seen another situation in which the seller immediately invested some of the proceeds in risky start-up companies (that ultimately died) without having a plan in place.

Your plan should consider the following:

Decide how to invest the proceeds to ensure that you will be able to obtain the same level of necessary income you had when you operated your business. Factor in your income from a salary if you have an earn-out situation.

If you have stock from the new company in the deal, decide if your portfolio is diversified enough for the risk of having a large amount of the new company stock.

If there is a tax liability associated with the deal, make sure that this, too, is factored into the financial plan.

Post-deal participation. Before completing the deal, make sure you have fully explored the probably post-deal environment. What does your relinquishment of control look like? Will you hold a board seat? Will you hold stock options? Will you have enough authority and/or control to be able to meet your earn-out goals and bonus targets?

If you are planning to be involved in the new organization or will have an equity stake in the company, make sure that all minute details are in writing. If you do not see the specific details in the definitive agreement, make sure to ask your lawyer before the deal closes. Sometimes it is not enough to trust that things will be the way you imagine they will be with the new company.

Escrow. When the deal closes, there is usually an escrow account that is established to "hold back" money from the seller to ensure that what the buyer has purchased is, in fact, what he or she got. This is the main remedy for the representations and warranties in the definitive agreement. Your goal as the seller is to have as little as possible in an escrow account. For one reason, when the money is in escrow account, the buyer will try to find any excuse to use this money to pay for normal business matters. I have seen situations in which cash from the deal, owed to the seller, literally sat in escrow for years because of a remote possibility of a lawsuit by former employees that had not even been raised by the former employees.

Press release. A press release is usually done by the acquiring company. However, before a press release goes out, make sure the buyer will not be disclosing any terms of the deal in any great detail, such that it's easy to calculate how much you, personally, will be receiving from the deal.

Do not bank in your head. As mentioned earlier, it is extremely important to keep focused on the business at hand and not start spending money before the deal closes. Keep only a very small circle of people in the know and try not to tell anybody until the deal closes and the cash is in your bank account. "It ain't over till it's over."

Handbook Questions:

- Have you analyzed and overanalyzed your company and personal tax situation before the close of the deal?
- Have you hired a financial planner and given thought to how you will invest your proceeds?
- Do you have an immediate plan for your proceeds after the deal closes?
- Have you evaluated the post-deal landscape and gotten in writing each minute detail?

CONCLUSION

Ask, and it shall be given to you; seek, and ye shall find; knock, and it shall be opened unto you.
—Matthew 7:7

I have worked with many companies over the years in helping to develop exit strategies, but the experience that sticks in my mind the most is the one mentioned in the introduction. Because everything went so wrong—incompatibility among team members, deadlines slipping, no plan B—I have carried the lessons learned when given an opportunity to create exit strategies for other companies.

This book has been a catalog of what steps should be taken, who you should hire to help, and what you can expect during the process of selling your business. My hope for the readers of this book is that they will have a successful and profitable exit from their company when the time is right, because they have learned from my experience.

This is the third handbook in the *Don't Be a Chicken* series. Although the subject of each book is different, ranging from starting a business to growing a business to planning an exit strategy, they all have one thing in common—a message of encouragement to go after your dreams and to take a chance on what may seem impossible. Most of all, this series asks you to trust yourself and God.

Because you picked up this book, you already have the drive to sell your company. Now you have the knowledge, so go ahead and ring that bell!

ABOUT THE AUTHOR

Douglas Palmer, author of *A Practical Handbook to Starting a Successful Business & A Practical Handbook to Growing Your Company…and Life at the Same Time* is an accomplished entrepreneur and business advisor. For over two decades, he has been a CPA and CFO serving large and small organizations both domestically and abroad. He has personally started multiple companies and now advises business owners. His firm has been in business for over a decade and has been the sponsor of the University of Maryland entrepreneurial programs. Doug also works with students on a pro bono basis.

Doug serves on numerous boards and is the chairman of St. John's Community Services Foundation, one of the oldest charities in Washington, DC.

Doug, his wife, Deborah, and their three children live in Maryland just outside of Washington, DC.

Appendix A

DUE DILIGENCE REQUEST LIST (EXAMPLE)

XIII. GENERAL CORPORATE MATERIALS

A. Minutes

1. Minutes of meetings of shareholders of the Company and its subsidiaries.

2. Minutes of meetings of the Board of Directors of the Company and its subsidiaries.

3. Minutes of meetings of committees, if any, of the Board of Directors of the Company and its subsidiaries.

4. Written Consents in lieu of items 1-3 above, if any.

B. Charter Documents

1. Articles or Certificate of Incorporation, as amended to date, of the Company and its subsidiaries.

2. Bylaws, as amended to date, of the Company and its subsidiaries.

3. List of jurisdictions in which the Company and its subsidiaries are qualified to do business or are otherwise operating and each jurisdiction in which the Company and its subsidiaries is licensed by any official or agency.

C. Organization

1. Organizational chart of the Company and its subsidiaries.

2. List of officers and directors of the Company and its subsidiaries.

3. List of the Company's shareholders. Indicate for each such shareholder the number of shares as to which such shareholder has (i) sole voting power; (ii) shared voting power; (iii) sole investment power or (iv) shared investment power. List of any entity engaged in the same industry as the Company, which is owned, in whole or in part, or operated by, or employs, any such individual.

4. A list of all corporations, partnerships, associations, joint ventures and other business entities in which the Company owns, directly or indirectly, an interest or any shares of capital stock. Such list shall include the nature of the interest, number of shares (if applicable), the percentage ownership of the Company in each such entity, the jurisdiction where each such entity was formed, each jurisdiction in which such entity is qualified to do business and the business presently conducted and, if different, proposed to be conducted by each entity.

D. Capital Stock

1. Securities authorized and outstanding (including stock books and records) for the Company and its subsidiaries.

2. Agreements, memoranda or registration statements relating to the acquisition, sale, issuance or attempted sale or issuance of securities.

3. Agreements relating to registration rights, voting of securities, preemptive rights, restrictive share transfers or similar matters.

4. The form(s) of the Company's Stock Certificates.

5. All warrants, warrant agreements, stock options or stock option agreements.

6. Schedule of option grants, including name of optionee, optionee's state of residence, date of grant, exercise

price, number of options granted, and number of options vested.

7.   Stockholder agreements, including voting agreements, voting trusts, proxies, stock purchase and repurchase agreements and stock restriction agreements.

8.   All other agreements or instruments, containing, constituting, or pertaining to commitments or rights relating to securities of the Company.

9.   All material communications to shareholders within the past five (5) years.

XIV.   FINANCIAL INFORMATION

A.   Consolidated financial statements, including accompanying schedules for the last five (5) years and the current fiscal year. Schedule providing a breakout by consulting engagement.

B.   Summary of major accounting policies, noting any which may be controversial or inconsistent with generally accepted accounting principles ("GAAP").

C.   Federal, state, local and foreign tax returns (including schedules and exhibits) filed by the Company for the last five (5) years. Schedule describing any ongoing tax disputes.

D. "S" Corporation election and any other tax elections, if applicable.

E. Schedule of all pending sales tax liabilities.

F. Copies of all IRS determination letters and all correspondence, including, without limitation, applications for private letter rulings and opinions of counsel, regarding the tax treatment of any transaction to which the Company is a party.

G. Reports of IRS auditors, state franchise tax auditors and related materials, including claims for refunds, investigations, audits or disputes, for any fiscal year not barred by the applicable statute of limitations.

H.   All management letters to the Company and all responses.

I. Internal financial plans, budgets and projections for the current year, with respect to the Company.

J.   List of all accounts receivable and accounts payable, in excess of $5,000, reflected on the balance sheet of the Company as of the most recent practicable date, specifying the name of each debtor or creditor, payment terms, the amount owing, and including an aging accounts receivable and accounts payable schedule. Schedule providing a breakout by consulting engagement.

K.   Schedule describing any liabilities of the Company or any subsidiary not disclosed in the latest balance sheet provided.

L.   Schedule of all assets under operating leases as of the latest balance sheet provided.

M.   Schedule of all assets under capitalized leases as of the latest balance sheet provided.

N.   Tangible assets ledger (e.g. fixed assets) as of the latest balance sheet provided.

O.   Schedule of major operational and accounting changes for the Company during the past five (5) years.

XV.   LITIGATION

A.   Schedule of all threatened or pending material litigation, claims or proceedings against or affecting the Company, and a description of any previous litigation that has been settled or finally adjudicated. Schedule should include name of proceeding, other parties, relief demanded and current status.

B.   All pleadings and correspondence relating to all pending or threatened litigation, claims and proceedings involving the Company or any of its subsidiaries as plaintiff or defendant.

C.   Consent decrees, settlement agreements and injunctions involving the Company or any of its subsidiaries.

D.   Letters from lawyers to the Company's auditors concerning litigation and other legal proceedings involving the Company or any of its subsidiaries during the last five (5) years.

E.   List of all agreements to which the Company is a party and which are in default.

F.   All correspondence and documents relating to the actual or alleged infringement of patents, trademarks or copyrights, or misuse or misappropriation of trade secrets.

G.   Any waivers or agreements canceling claims or rights of substantial value other than in the ordinary course of business.

XVI.   COMPLIANCE WITH LAWS

A.   A schedule setting forth all governmental agencies to which the Company or any subsidiary reports.

B.   Governmental permits, licenses and consents.

C.   Schedule of contracts with the United States government or any agency or contractor thereof.

D.   Correspondence and notices relating to contracts with any governmental entity (by the Company directly or indirectly or through any prime contractor, subcontractor or vendor) to the extent related to: (a) any alleged violation or omission, (b) any negative determinations of responsibility issued against the Company with respect to any bid, quotation or proposal submitted by the company, (c) any disallowance or questioning by the federal government of material costs incurred by the Company, any assessment of penalties or damages of any kind against the Company arising out of any material irregularities, misstatements or omissions relating to any of the Company's contracts, bids, quotations or proposals, past or present, (d) any audit, and (e) any denial of security clearances and permits necessary for the execution of the Company's obligations under any contract, past or present.

E. Citations and notices received from any federal, state, local or foreign governmental agencies. Summary of any pending or threatened OSHA, EPA or Department of Labor inquiries or proceedings.

F. All communications to and other filings with any federal, state, local or foreign governmental agencies during the last five (5) years.

G. Any reports, notices or correspondence relating to any purported violation or infringement by the Company or any of its subsidiaries.

XVII. PERSONNEL

A. List of all current employees of the Company and any subsidiaries, including a brief job description, current rate of compensation and start date for each such employee. Management turnover information for the past five (5) years.

B. All collective bargaining agreements, employment agreements and non-competition agreements.

C. Management and employment contracts, including severance agreements, indemnification agreements and agreements not to compete.

D. Consulting contracts with third parties (including expired agreements) during last five (5) years.

E. Employee benefit, pension, health, deferred compensation and profit-sharing plans or programs, including trust instruments, plan summaries, financial statements and plan evaluations for the most recent plan year and most recent actuarial evaluation.

F. All 401(k) plan documents, including but not limited to:

1. Plan Document

2. Adoption Agreement (if Plan is a prototype)

3. Trust Agreement

4. Summary Plan Description

5. Most recent IRS determination letter

6. Any Plan amendments since the date of the most recent IRS determination letter

7. Forms 5500 for past 3 Plan years

8. Nondiscrimination testing for past 3 Plan years

G. Stock ownership plans, stock option and stock appreciation rights plans, phantom stock plans, incentive stock option plans, bonus plans or similar arrangements, and a schedule of the salaries of executive officers of the Company and its subsidiaries.

H. Loans and guarantees to or from directors, officers or employees of the Company and its subsidiaries.

I. Indemnification agreements with any employee or director.

J. Copies of personnel policies, personnel manuals and employee handbooks.

XVIII. PROPERTY

A. List of all offices and facilities.

B. Copies of mortgages on all "property, plant and equipment" owned by the Company or any subsidiary.

C. Copies of all documents evidencing title to real property owned by the Company, its subsidiaries and any affiliated partnership and copies of policies of title insurance or title searches relating thereto.

D. Leases and related agreements for all "property, plant and equipment" used or owned by the Company or any subsidiary.

E. Copies of contracts and options to purchase or sell real property or to construct improvements thereon.

F.   All material equipment purchase agreements.

F.   List of all liens or encumbrances against real and personal property.

G.   Schedule and brief description of intellectual property and intangible assets and any pending applications therefor and ownership documents relating thereto, including but not limited to (1) all U.S. or foreign patents and patent applications, (2) all U.S. or foreign trademarks, service marks and tradenames, whether registered or unregistered, and (3) all U.S. or foreign copyrights, registered or unregistered, and (4) all other intangible assets.

H.   Any appraisals of the Company's real property obtained within the past five (5) years.

I.   Systems information, including infrastructure, model and age of key systems, technical platforms used, and financial and project management systems.

XIX.   RISK MANAGEMENT/INSURANCE

A.   Schedule of all insurance policies in force including policy periods, limits, and premiums.

B.   Copies of current workers compensation, property and general liability insurance policies.

C.   List of material claims filed within the last five (5) years.

XX.   FINANCING

All material loan agreements, including, but not limited to:

A.   Short term and long term debt (including capitalized leases, indentures, mortgages, notes, agreements, guarantees and other contingent liabilities).

B.   Credit agreements, loan agreements, promissory notes, revolving lines of credit and indentures.

C.   Mortgages, trust agreements and security agreements.

D. All agreements with respect to obligations or liabilities as guarantor, surety, co-signer, endorser, co-maker, indemnitor or otherwise in respect of the obligation of any other person.

E. All agreements by which the Company is subject to any obligation to provide funds to or to make investments in any other person (in the form of a loan, capital contribution or otherwise).

F. Schedule of all security interests that relate directly or indirectly to the assets or to the conduct of the Company, along with copies of security agreements and financing statements relating thereto. The schedule should list all assets subject to liens.

G. All material correspondence with and from lenders in the past five (5) years, including, without limitation, compliance letters and notices of default or potential default with respect to any material loan agreements, credit agreements or guarantees, including waivers and related correspondence

H. Any agreement with any broker or agent.

XXI. OPERATIONAL MATTERS AND OTHER MATERIAL AGREEMENTS

A. All agreements or plans for mergers, consolidations, reorganizations, acquisitions or the purchase or sale of assets involving the Company or any subsidiary, whether consummated or not, and all agreements with federal, state and local regulatory agencies entered into in connection with such transactions.

B. All consulting engagement agreements for the past five (5) years.

C. Marketing agreements, including sales agent or representative, dealer and distributor agreements, reseller agreements, consignment and pricing agreements.

D. Long-term service contracts, including any future or anticipated contracts.

E. Joint venture and partnership agreements.

F. License and royalty agreements.

G. VAR, VAD, OEM and similar agreements.

H.   Management, service and tax-sharing agreements.

I. Contracts outside the ordinary course of business.

J.   Agreements with management or key personnel other than employment or consulting agreements.

K.   Schedule describing all material transactions involving the Company or any subsidiary and (i) any officer or director, (ii) any other affiliate (including 5% stockholders) of the Company or any subsidiary, or (iii) any entity owned, in whole or in part, by any officer, director or stockholder, and any agreements pertaining to the foregoing, which are not reflected in the items heretofore listed.

L.   Secrecy, confidentiality, non-compete and non-disclosure agreements with employees or third parties.

L.   Any contract purporting to limit the Company's business activities or ability to compete in any market.

M.   Any other material contracts.

XXII.   <u>CUSTOMERS AND SUPPLIERS</u>

A.   Copies of all outstanding agreements with customers and suppliers, including any service, support or maintenance agreements, involving annual revenues or expenses in excess of $10,000.

B.   List of the Company's top 30 customers (including addresses and telephone numbers, if possible), and, if possible, a breakdown by revenue per customer.

C.   List of the Company's top 20 suppliers (including addresses and telephone numbers, if possible), and, if available, a breakdown by purchases per supplier. Please indicate any sole-source supplier.

D.   Any form contract or license used with supplier or customers, including form license agreement and support/maintenance agreement

XXIII. ENVIRONMENTAL

A.   Previous environmental assessments.

B.   All pending or existing environmental permits, licenses or other governmental approvals and all enforcement-related documents.

C.   Governmental requests for environmental or health and safety studies and the responses thereto by the Company or any subsidiary.

D.   Known or suspected environmental problems, including those associated with neighboring or related property.

E.   Agreements or financing documents with provisions relating to environmental conditions or liabilities. These would include warranties, representations, indemnities, escrow agreements, etc.

F.   Insurance policies which cover liability for environmental impairment.

XXIV. INTELLECTUAL PROPERTY

A.   Copies of all existing material licenses or sublicenses (including any VARs or VADs) to which the Company is a party, either as a licensor or licensee. Also, include all existing material contracts or leases conveying to the Company rights regarding any facility, equipment or other material asset or service used in or relating to the Company's business.

B.   All material patent, copyright and intellectual property agreements, including research and/or development agreements, to which the Company is a party.

C.   Documents relating to any claims of infringement of intellectual property rights of others.

D.   List and copies of all patents and applications pending, held or being prosecuted by the Company in the United States or elsewhere, with descriptive titles, numbers, jurisdiction, and copies of all correspondence to or from examining authorities or other parties regarding such patents and patent applications.

E.   List and copies of all copyright registrations and applications pending, held or being prosecuted by the Company in the United States or elsewhere, with descriptive titles, numbers, jurisdiction, and a list of all copyrightable materials (including software and documentation) material to the Company's business, as to which there is no copyright registration or application therefor pending.

F.   List and copies of all trademarks, registered or unregistered, used in connection with the business of the Company, whether or not such trademarks are owned by or licensed to the Company, with a description of products or services associated therewith, and numbers, jurisdiction, status of any registration applications pending, if any, and copies of all state and federal registration and recordation documents and certifications pertaining to each (including associated affidavits).

G.   List of all items and categories of technology (whether or not patented or patentable) that are material to the business of the Company, together with a brief description of how each such technology was developed or acquired.

H.   Copies of all agreements pursuant to which the Company has assigned any technology or intellectual property rights to, or obtained any technology or intellectual property rights from, third parties.

I.   Copies of all agreements pursuant to which the Company's products are distributed or marketed by third parties.

J.   Copies of all agreements pursuant to which the Company's products are manufactured or assembled by, or pursuant to which the Company acquires products or components for products from, third parties.

K.   Copies of all research and development agreements to which the Company is a party.

L.   Copies of all other agreements relating to technology or intellectual property that are material to the business of the Company.

M.   List of engineers and other employees who have participated or contributed in a material way to the development of the Company's intellectual property, a brief description of their roles, and copies of their resumes or other evidence of previous job history.

N.   Copies of the Company's standard form of agreement with employees and independent contractors regarding confidentiality, non-disclosure, and assignment of inventions, and a list of all employees and all independent contractors who have executed the agreements, and a list of all employees and all independent contractors who have not executed the agreements.

O.   Copies of confidentiality, non-disclosure, and assignment of invention agreements, between the Company and employees, and between the Company and independent contractors the contents of which differ from those set forth in the standard form.

P.   Copies of the Company's standard form of confidentiality and non-disclosure agreements, between the Company and persons or organizations other than employees and independent contractors, and a list of persons or organization who have executed the agreements.

Q.   Copies of confidentiality and non-disclosure agreements, between the Company and persons or organizations other than employees and independent contractors, the contents of which differ from those set forth in the standard form.

R.   All documents, correspondence, memos, notes, and other papers relating to the Company's written policies on intellectual property.

S.   Copies of all security agreements pursuant to which a lender or creditor has taken a security interest in specific intellectual property assets or "general intangibles."

T.   Uniform commercial code filings, or other state and federal filings, that relate in any way to any of the Company's technology or intellectual property.

U.   All documents, correspondence, pleadings, memos, notes, and other papers relating to any pending or threatened intellectual property litigation or claim against the Company, or any other assertion, suggestion, or inquiry by a third party that the Company is infringing its intellectual property rights.

V.   Flow charts, technical specifications, and other design documents relating to any company technology or product that is the subject of any pending or threatened litigation, claim, assertion, suggestion, or inquiry of the type described in item U above.

W.   Materials referred to during the process of developing any Company technology or product that is the subject of any pending or threatened litigation, claim, assertion, suggestion, or inquiry or the type described in item U above.

X.   Journal articles, published papers, and textbooks relating to any Company technology or product that is the subject of any pending or threatened litigation, claim, assertion, suggestion, or inquiry or the type described in item U above.

Y.   Notes of design meetings relating to any Company technology or product that is the subject of any pending or threatened litigation, claim, assertion, suggestion, or inquiry or the type described in item U above.

Z.   All documents, correspondence, memos, notes, and other papers relating to any development by the Company that involves the derivation or use of specifications or technical information derived from the products of third parties, including without limitation any "clean room" development efforts.

AA.   All documents, correspondence, memos, notes, and other papers analyzing or assessing the validity or scope of any Company copyright, patent, or trademark.

BB.   A list or inventory of all trade secrets and know-how of the Company or its subsidiaries that are owned or used by the Company or its subsidiaries.

CC.   A list or inventory of any intellectual property rights that the Company or its subsidiaries does not legally own or does not have a legal right to use, but that are required for the Company or its subsidiaries to carry on its existing businesses, product lines and services.

XXV. MISCELLANEOUS

A.   Disclosure documents used in any public or private placements, bond financings, or institutional or bank loan applications.

B.   All press releases, articles and brochures issued by or relating to the Company or any subsidiary.

C.   Copies of documents relating to acquisitions or divestitures involving the Company, its assets or securities (other than in the ordinary course) during last 5 years or currently pending and any information as to plans regarding future acquisitions or divestitures.

D.   Copies of all consultants' reports prepared with respect to the operations of the Company within the last five (5) years.

E.   All business plans and other strategy documents.

F.   All other documents and information which, in the company's judgment, are significant with respect to any portion of its business or which should be considered and reviewed in making disclosures regarding the business and financial condition of the Company to prospective investors.